♥ **THIS JOURNAL BELONGS TO** ♥

_____

The Just Girl Project

Self-Love

JOURNAL

ILANA HARKAVY

ILLUSTRATIONS BY ERICA LEWIS

SPRUCE BOOKS
A.Sasquatch Books Imprint

CONTENTS

BEFORE JOURNALING | AFTER JOURNALING

INTRODUCTION

HEY, GIRL!

It's been a minute! Last time we spoke you were obviously reading *The Just Girl Project Book of Self-Care*. A great read, I must say. And OMG, you're doing amazing! Looking beautiful and strong, flexing those self-care muscles. You must be proud of yourself, for real. I know I'm proud of you!

Okay, so story time: When I was a young girl, making friends did NOT come easily to me. I always felt like an outsider, longing for meaningful connections. I mean, I listened to a lot of Backstreet Boys. It wasn't until I started writing that everything changed for me. I finally found a way to connect with myself, and that was meaningful.

And then something wondrous happened: I met my first close and personal friend. Her name was Daisy, then Anabelle, then Sparkles . . . she liked to change it up. What did she look like? Well, she was pretty bold and so on-trend. Lavender velvet, Hello Kitty, vintage florals, denim. She had THE COOLEST style. The best part was that she knew ALL my secrets, worries, and fears, but she kept them safe, under lock and key. And she never judged, just listened, allowing me to divulge my deepest desires without abandon.

She was, of course, My Diary. A notebook filled with pages of imagination and vulnerability. A midnight train to dreamland, words flying through me like pixie dust. And I reveled in the adventure, writing to her every single day. When we moved from California to Seattle and my world imploded, there she was: cuddled up with me and my flashlight under my comforter as the rain poured, tears streamed down my face, and I wrote about a place called Elsewhere. Or at summer camp, when kids were running round the field or jumping in the pool, there I was with my bestie: resting on a rainbow beach towel, popsicle in hand, giggling as the sun kissed my cheeks. I wrote to her about embarrassments, crushes, opinions, my first taste of relationships and drama. My diary knew me better than anyone, and it was the best feeling to have her by my side.

But then as I got older, my life expanded and I ventured out of my little bubble, her pages began to gather dust, and my dreamy hobby became a thing of the past.

It wasn't until college that I learned grown-ups had diaries too. They were called *journals*, and they were all the rage in self-exploration and self-care. I remember buying my first adult journal—a beautiful pink Moleskine with the words Dream Now on the cover. I opened it up, tracing its pages with my fingers and worrying that the words wouldn't come to me as easily as before. I closed my eyes, took a deep breath, and told myself, "Just write." And it worked. I got back to poetry, songwriting, recording painful memories from heartbreak and happy ones from my travels abroad. It felt like the words had never left me.

So now that I've shared my very romantic journey of journaling with you, let's cut to it!

Simply put, journaling is the act of writing things down. And it's damn POWERFUL. Journaling offers the perfect retreat from the chaos of our everyday lives—an opportunity to slow down and focus, resolve problems, and channel our creative energy.

Our human brains are legit. Our capacity to memorize spans terabytes, but with the deluge of new info every day, all too often we forget the details. Journals allow us to record what we want to remember, reminding us what's important (or what was important to us at the time). Journaling is the ultimate way to help our minds sift through all the chaos and focus on what's emotionally true and which details are really important, allowing us to make better choices, solve problems, and visualize what we want our future to look like. So let's dive in deeper and look at all the gifts that journaling offers!

IT BOOSTS YOUR MOOD

Bottling up your feelings can take a BIG toll on your mental health. Journaling is a great way to identify and describe what you are feeling, address those feelings, and reflect on them. This simple act can help you really understand what is going on with yourself and switch from a negative to a positive mindset. There are even lots of studies that show that daily writing exercises, such as making notes about what you're thankful for, can help reinforce feelings of happiness.

IT REDUCES STRESS

Anxiety is kind of the worst for your mental health, making it hard to focus on anything else. Luckily, journaling is an incredible tool for managing stress. Expressing your worries consistently in writing helps you manage your anxiety in a healthy way. I love writing in my journal before bed, whenever my mind starts to race, or when I wake up in the morning. Getting my wildest thoughts and dreams out of my system helps me unwind and relax. Because just like our bodies, our brains need a little exercise and release.

IT KEEPS YOUR MEMORY SHARP

I'm a big fan of physical journals (like ours, obvi) because writing things down by hand helps your brain process your thoughts more clearly and commit them to memory more easily. Journaling makes you pay attention— it gets your mind to really focus on something—and because of the nature of memory, you're more likely to remember the things you focus on.

IT SUPERCHARGES YOUR EMOTIONAL HEALTH

When you regularly connect with your own self, you become more attuned to your needs and desires. You're able to stay present while reflecting and processing your emotions—what's called mindfulness, and it's a great way to self-regulate. You get to acknowledge and reflect upon your patterns, helping you grow and feel more confident. It's like researching yourself. You develop this super in-depth report on yourself and how you interact with the world. Once you start to do that, you'll unlock memories and ideas—not to mention confidence—giving you full access to your brainpower. So you'll pretty much be a superhero.

And . . . the BIGGEST reason: TAYLOR SWIFT JOURNALS!

Yes, in fact, Taylor has been journaling ever since she could put pen to paper. Her juicy Grammy award–winning diary entries should absolutely serve as inspiration for you.

So now you totally get it! Journaling is catharsis at its finest. But if you're like me and often find yourself staring at those blank pages, feeling lost, scared, alone, and kind of like, "Okay, journal, tell me what to write today and please solve all my problems," you've come to the right place. Because this is a Just Girl Project journal. And JGP doesn't believe in leaving you hanging to fend for yourself. No, we're here to guide you, to give you the deep, sophisticated stuff you've been needing in your life.

Within this guided journal you'll find fun, inviting prompts accompanied by adorable colorful illustrations featuring tips, quotes, and exercises to boost your emotional and physical well-being. With each page, you'll lean into self-knowledge and creative expression. This journal is here to inspire you to write down your feelings, self-reflections, creative ideas, and plans for making your dreams come true.

But first things first: Take that deep breath, close your eyes, and tell yourself, "I need to do this for me." You really need to take a moment every day to reflect and express yourself. And journaling is the best way to do it. So break out your pencils (or if you're like me, pastel gel pens) and get to it! This isn't a place to judge yourself for poor grammar or spelling errors. This is a time to be raw, honest, and vulnerable. This is for YOU, and you only. So have fun with it!

xoxo,

TIPS FOR JOURNALING

CUSTOMIZE + DECORATE YOUR JOURNAL.

KEEP A LIST OF PROMPTS READY.

THINK OF IT AS A WAY TO UNWIND. THE ACT OF WRITING > THE ACTUAL WORDS.

CLOSE YOUR EYES AND REFLECT ON YOUR DAY. WRITE ABOUT WHAT COMES TO MIND.

SET A TIMER TO HELP YOU STAY FOCUSED.

THERE ARE NO RULES—YOU DECIDE WHAT JOURNALING LOOKS LIKE FOR YOU.

Loving Myself (for Who I Am)

Sometimes we are so focused on getting others to love us that we forget to love ourselves! But the truth is, you can't have a healthy relationship with anyone else until you have one with yourself. So this chapter is about getting to know and love yourself.

Once I've laced up my combat boots, I feel like I can take on anything. What items from your closet make you feel like a badass?

My Nike sneakers and my american eagle jeans, with the makeup on

CONFIDENCE STARTER PACK

DOC
MARTENS

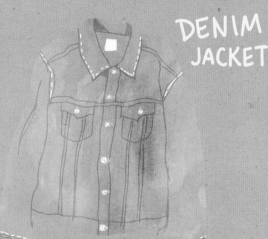

DENIM
JACKET

COLD
BREW

CO-STAR
APP

4 Main Personality Types

TYPE A
- uses time wisely
- is a go-getter
- competitive
- organized
- rational
- assertive
- impatient

TYPE B

- relaxed
- peaceful
- grounded
- patient
- easygoing
- has a calming influence on peo
- procrastinates

TYPE C

- perfectionistic
- detail-oriented
- needs a routine
- reserved
- organized
- is a people-pleaser
- follows the rules
- logical

TYPE D

- sensitive
- introspective
- anxious
- existential
- emotional
- realistic
- experiences more negative emotions
- pessimistic
- resilient

Which one are you? It's okay if you've got qualities from multiple personality types—make a list below and see if you're leaning into one or if you're a combo of several. Remember, it's not about judging yourself—the idea is to recognize your personality traits and get to know yourself!

I definitly have a Type-C personality! This trait perfectly describes me.

Are you hard on yourself? Mindful self-compassion, or the practice of being kind to yourself, is a much better path to getting what you need. What are some ways that you can treat yourself with kindness?

Being patient with myself when things do not go as planned.

what we think:

"I NEED TO BE MEAN + CRITICAL OF MYSELF SO THAT I CAN IMPROVE AND GROW."

what is actually true:

"I HAVE TO TAKE RISKS AND PUT MYSELF OUT THERE TO GROW, AND I CAN'T DO THAT WITHOUT LOVING AND BELIEVING IN MYSELF THE WAY I AM."

Self-Love Reminders

You are worthy of so much love, whether or not you are in a relationship.

It's normal to feel like you don't know what you're doing.

It's okay to res and take breaks

A day spent relaxing and checking in on your mental health is not a day wasted.

You're your own kind of beautiful; you don't need to be like anyone else.

Most of us have an inner critic—a voice inside that tells us we are not measuring up. Don't listen! What are some supportive things you can say to yourself to cancel out the voice of your inner critic?

_____

_____

_____

_____

_____

_____

_____

_____

_____

_____

_____

_____

_____

_____

_____

_____

_____

_____

_____

_____

Positive affirmations are great for boosting confidence, so you want to have some ready when you need them! Can you come up with five personally effective affirmations that you can use when you're feeling unsure of yourself?

POSITIVE AFFIRMATIONS

HOW ARE YOU FEELING?	YOUR AFFIRMATION
 TIRED	It's okay to say no or ask for help.
NERVOUS	I have everything I need to get through this. I am strong.
 OVERWHELMED	I am confident in my ability to make the right decisions.
FINE...	I am creating the life of my dreams.
SAD	I am not my negative thoughts.

Knowing who you are and asking others to acknowledge your truth is your right as a human, and though it shouldn't require courage to just be you, it often does. Are there aspects of yourself that you have not shared but that you would you like to share with others? How can you get there?

Write about something positive that you can do for yourself this week—
give details about how and when you're going to do it, and imagine how
this act of self-love is going to make you feel good.

Self-Love Tips

UNFOLLOWING
PEOPLE WHO
MAKE YOU FEEL BAD
ABOUT YOURSELF

DECLUTTERING
YOUR MIND

CUTTING OFF
TOXIC PEOPLE

TAKING A LONG
AND RELAXING
BATH

THINKING OF THIS
TIME AS A
BEAUTIFUL NEW
BEGINNING

WHAT I'M THINKING AND FEELING RIGHT NOW

Why talking about your mental health struggles helps

YOU'LL FEEL SUPPORTED AND LESS ALONE

YOU CAN BETTER UNDERSTAND WHAT'S GOING ON IN YOUR HEAD

YOU MIGHT UNCOVER NEW THOUGHTS AND FEELINGS WHILE TALKING ABOUT YOUR EXPERIENCES

YOU CAN MAKE A PLAN SO YOU CAN GET THE HELP YOU NEED

Keeping My Head Together

Truth: No human being has perfect mental health all the time! Everyone has issues. In this chapter, we are going to explore some of the common mental and emotional challenges we experience and practice good coping skills.

How can you stop yourself from overthinking? Acknowledge that you're doing it, then pause and write down your thoughts. Let it all out, then look at what you've written and challenge each thought by coming up with a different way to look at it.

THE CYCLE OF OVERTHINKING

1 OVERTHINK SOMETHING

2 BECOME ANXIOUS

3 GET OVERWHELMED BY A SWARM OF IDEAS BUT STILL HAVE NO ANSWERS

4 I NEED TO THINK ABOUT THIS SOME MORE!

THINGS NO ONE TELLS YOU ABOUT ANXIETY

IT'S WORSE AT NIGHT

IT CAN CAUSE PHYSICAL SYMPTOMS- HEADACHES, BODY ACHES, DIGESTIVE ISSUES, ETC

SOMETIMES IT MAKES US ANGRY AND LASH OUT

IT CAN BE EXHAUSTING

IT'S UNPREDICTABLE

IT'S THE NUMBER-ONE MENTAL HEALTH COMPLAINT IN THE WORLD

YOU ALWAYS FEEL GUILTY OR LIKE YOU'VE DONE SOMETHING WRONG

Anxiety is extremely common—and extremely uncomfortable! Writing down your worries helps because finding the words to describe your feelings turns on the rational part of your brain and dials down the anxious part. Write down five things you're anxious about—you'll feel better after.

Panic attacks can make you feel like you're gonna die! But you're not, I promise. Panicky feelings, though intense, are just feelings. Try writing down three or four calming sentences that you can use when you are freaking out to remind you that this will pass and you will be okay.

HOW TO CALM YOURSELF DURING A PANIC ATTACK

Focus on an object — stare at the item and think about how it looks, feels, its shape, color, etc.

Take deep, slow breaths. Count to 4 seconds on the inhale and 8 seconds on the exhale.

Move to a peaceful and quiet place if possible.

Remind yourself that what you are experiencing is anxiety, not a real danger.

TYPES OF INTRUSIVE THOUGHTS

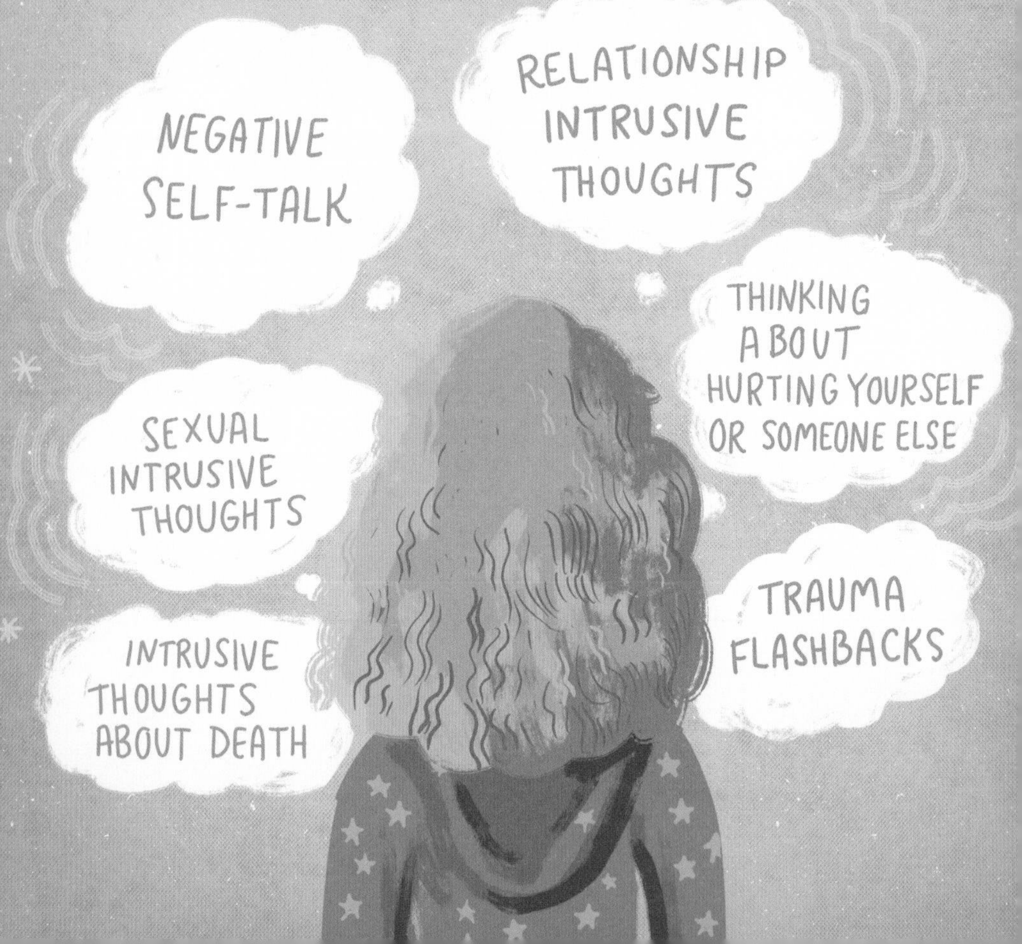

Not every thought in your head is worth keeping—when you have an intrusive thought, instead of thinking of it as a messenger of truth, acknowledge that it's just noise and let it go. Jot down three thoughts that upset you, and then next to each one, write why it is false or meaningless.

Depression is a liar! When you feel depression's negativity creeping in, write down five things you feel grateful for in your life.

What Toxic Positivity looks like

FEELING GUILT OR SHAME FOR FEELING, DOWN, BECAUSE SOMEONE ELSE HAS IT WORSE

"JUST LOOK ON THE BRIGHT SIDE"

"JUST GET OVER IT"

HIDING HOW YOU REALLY FEEL (FROM OTHERS AND YOURSELF)

ONLY SHARING THE GOOD MOMENTS ON SOCIAL MEDIA

FOCUSING ONLY ON THE POSITIVES AND REJECTING THE NEGATIVES

You can't really feel happy unless you also sometimes feel sad. Every life—and even every day—has both good and bad moments! Toxic positivity is just a form of fear, and it steals your ability to acknowledge important feelings like sadness, regret, melancholy, or grief. Describe a sad feeling you had that was appropriate and necessary.

If you've been bullied, it probably made you feel terrible, even worthless. Counter those feelings by writing down three things that you like about yourself or that you're good at.

_____

_____

_____

_____

_____

_____

_____

_____

_____

_____

_____

_____

_____

_____

_____

_____

_____

_____

_____

_____

Bullying made me feel...

SCARED

POWERLESS

EMBARRASSED

LIKE A
FAILURE

ANXIOUS

SMALL

INSECURE

ALONE

WEAK

ANGRY

UNSAFE

When you're feeling lonely

CONNECT WITH
PEOPLE ONLINE
+ IRL

DON'T BLAME
YOURSELF

READ A
BOOK

KNOW YOU
AREN'T ALONE
IN FEELING
LONELY

JOURNAL
AND WRITE
YOUR FEELINGS
DOWN

PLAY WITH
A PET!

MAKE PLANS
WITH FRIENDS
FOR THE FUTURE
TO HAVE SOMETHING
TO LOOK FORWARD TO

LISTEN TO
A PODCAST

Everyone feels alone sometimes—that is part of being human. Instead of dwelling on those sad feelings, acknowledge that you really are not totally alone and describe a recent moment when you felt connected to a friend, family member, or even someone you just met!

List your top five sad songs. Next to each song title, explain how it actually makes you feel better!

Why listening to sad music helps

It helps us understand and put words to our feelings

It gives us a healthy outlet for our emotions

It triggers nostalgic memories

It releases dopamine and improves mood

It can make us feel less alone in our struggles

It makes us reflect on our own experiences and feel comforted

Why rewatching shows/movies helps

We know how they will make us feel, so we can use them to regulate our emotions

They require less mental energy

When we're dealing with uncertainty, they can bring us predictability + safety

They bring back happy memories of the first time we watched them

Jot down your fave shows to watch over and over again.
Which ones work best for which situations?

Choosing healthy activities—the kind you know will make you feel calmer, happier, and more connected—is a great way to practice being good to yourself. Make a list of five things to do that are good for you.

INSTEAD OF THIS,
TRY THIS:

Scrolling your phone before bed → Read a book until your eyes get tired

Keeping your thoughts and stresses to yourself → Ask for help and let someone else in

Gossiping and speaking badly about others → Find friends who you can talk to for hours without needing to tear others down

Feeling overwhelmed by too many tasks → Take 5 minutes to clean your space

Procrastinating on the projects that stress you out → Try to figure out the real reason you keep putting it off. Does it trigger negative thoughts?

WHAT I'M THINKING AND FEELING RIGHT NOW

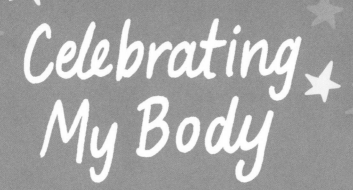

Celebrating My Body

Girl, you know that you are beautiful—not because your body looks a certain way but because it's yours—unique, amazing, and brilliant. Being comfortable with your body is a superpower that you can learn. Let's talk about how to feel good in your body.

Practicing body neutrality—accepting and appreciating your body for what it is—can be easier than trying to love everything about how you look all the time. Practice this way of thinking by coming up with a few body-neutral statements that are purely descriptive, like "my legs are muscular" or "my skin protects me."

Body Positivity

Body Neutrality

All people should be able to love their bodies as they are.

Love your body for how it looks.

Your body is beautiful regardless of what society says.

Your appearance shouldn't determine your value.

Instead of focusing on how your body looks, focus on what your body does for you.

Loving your body is hard, and that's ok. You don't have to love the way you look all the time.

Helpful <u>Body-Neutral</u> Affirmations

I am more than a body.

My happiness is not dependent on how attractive I am to others.

I don't need to change my body.

I don't need to LOVE how I look all the time in order to feel good about myself.

My body will change many times throughout my life, and that's ok.

My body is the least interesting thing about me.

Okay, I am not sure I'm ever going to loooove my body—but I can definitely get comfortable with it, appreciate it, and stop obsessing over how I look. You can do that too! Jot down five things you truly appreciate about your body and what it does for you.

Let's trash the scale and just forget about the numbers. Write down five things you like about yourself that have nothing to do with how much you weigh or how you look.

your weight is literally just a number!

Things that help me feel better about my body

Following people with similar bodies to mine on social media

Knowing that stretch marks, cellulite, acne, etc. are perfectly normal and nothing to hide

Avoiding the scale – numbers are just numbers!

Wearing clothes that make me feel confident, comfortable, and <u>myself</u>

Learning how diet culture profits from our insecurities

News flash! No body is perfect. But every body is a marvel. Make a list of people you admire whose bodies do not fit the "perfect" image.

Write a love letter to your body just the way it is. Tell your body how you're going to take good care of it.

_____

_____

_____

_____

_____

_____

_____

_____

_____

_____

_____

_____

_____

_____

_____

_____

_____

_____

How to befriend your body

exercise to feel good, not to create a different body

honor its feelings— rest when your body needs it

et it shine n the outfits ou love

write a love letter to your body the way it is right now

give it the nutrients it needs to thrive

Why I love food

Food is fuel!
It gives me the
energy I need to enjoy
my day

Food = comfort
Certain foods bring
back memories and
make me feel relaxed

My personal taste an
food choices help me
express myself

Food brings people
together

Guess what? Food is not good or bad—it's just food. The trick is to figure out the food that works best for *you*. Make a list of ten food items that taste good to you, give you energy, and do not give you any digestive troubles.

One of the best ways to make friends with your body is to figure out the kinds of activities that feel good to you. List some of the ways that you like to move your body.

Why I love my body

hating my body makes me feel much worse

it's unique— no one's body is exactly like mine

the process of learning to love my body is so much more rewarding

my body has carried me through so much and deserves to be celebrated

How to practice age positivity

reframe your thoughts—
wrinkles = reminders of
all the times you laughed

it's such a waste
of time to compare
your body with
how it used to
look— change is
normal!

don't fall for
the unrealistic
expectations
set by celebrities
and photoshop

don't punish your
body for doing
what it's supposed
to do as you
get older

Getting older means getting better! List some of the good things you think age will bring you, like confidence, wisdom, and perspective.

The mirror is not your enemy or your friend—it's just a tool for reflecting. So use it to reflect on what's positive about what you see. Write down five nice things to say when you see yourself.

Nice things to say to yourself in the mirror

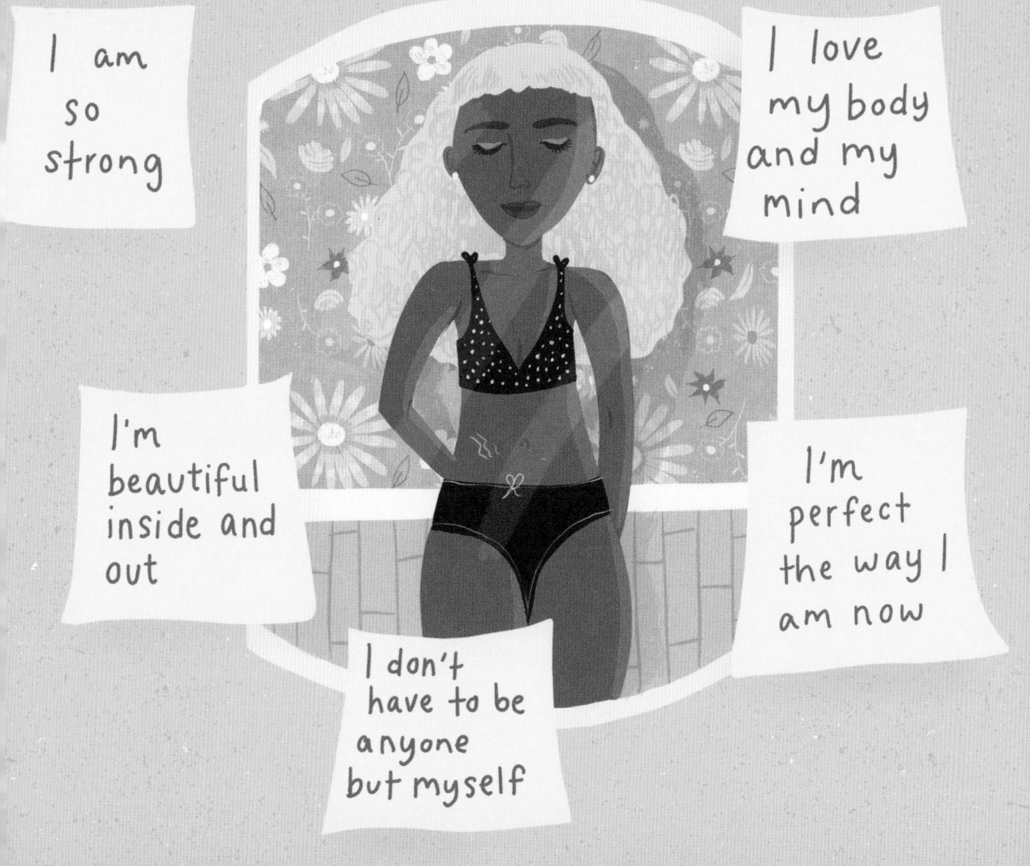

WHAT I'M THINKING AND FEELING RIGHT NOW

Unrealistic Expectations TV Shows gave me about family

every conflict gets resolved after one big fight or getting "grounded"

families eat a full breakfast together every single morning

dad is always funny and likable while mom is mean and uptight

everyone is always hanging out at home

one sibling is preppy and popular while the other is an outcast/artist

someone in your family will read your diary

My Family Ties

Family can be . . . complicated.
Figuring out how to deal and exist in
your family will take a lifetime, but
it is always worth it. Let's get past
expectations and spend some time
on our real family dynamics.

Do you recognize any of these traits in yourself? What influence (if any) do you think your place in the birth order has had on how you relate to the world—or to your siblings?

_____

_____

_____

_____

_____

_____

_____

_____

_____

_____

_____

_____

_____

_____

_____

_____

_____

_____

_____

Oldest child things

- parents are more strict with you
- desire to overachieve
- bossy
- feel pressure to set a good example

Middle child things

- agreeable and diplomatic
- independent
- used to having to speak up to be heard
- strong social skills

Youngest child things

- carefree
- more rebellious
- you seem older than you really are
- outgoing
- can get away with things your sibling(s) could not

Only child things

- mature
- creative
- self-entertainer
- care a lot about friendships
- avoid conflict
- feel pressure to please parents
- love making new friends

Sibling Things

Borrowing or stealing each other's
things without asking

Fighting one minute and being
best friends the next

Gossiping with them about
family drama

Always comparing
yourself to them

Telling each other things you would
never tell anyone else

Sibling relationships are unique and special. Are there moments, memories, or stories that truly capture the bond between you and your siblings?

I know it's hard, but boundaries actually make things better. List three boundaries you want to set with your family, and try out some scripts for making them happen. ("I love you and I promise to let you know if I'm dating someone serious, but I need you to stop asking every time I see you.")

Why it's hard to set boundaries with family

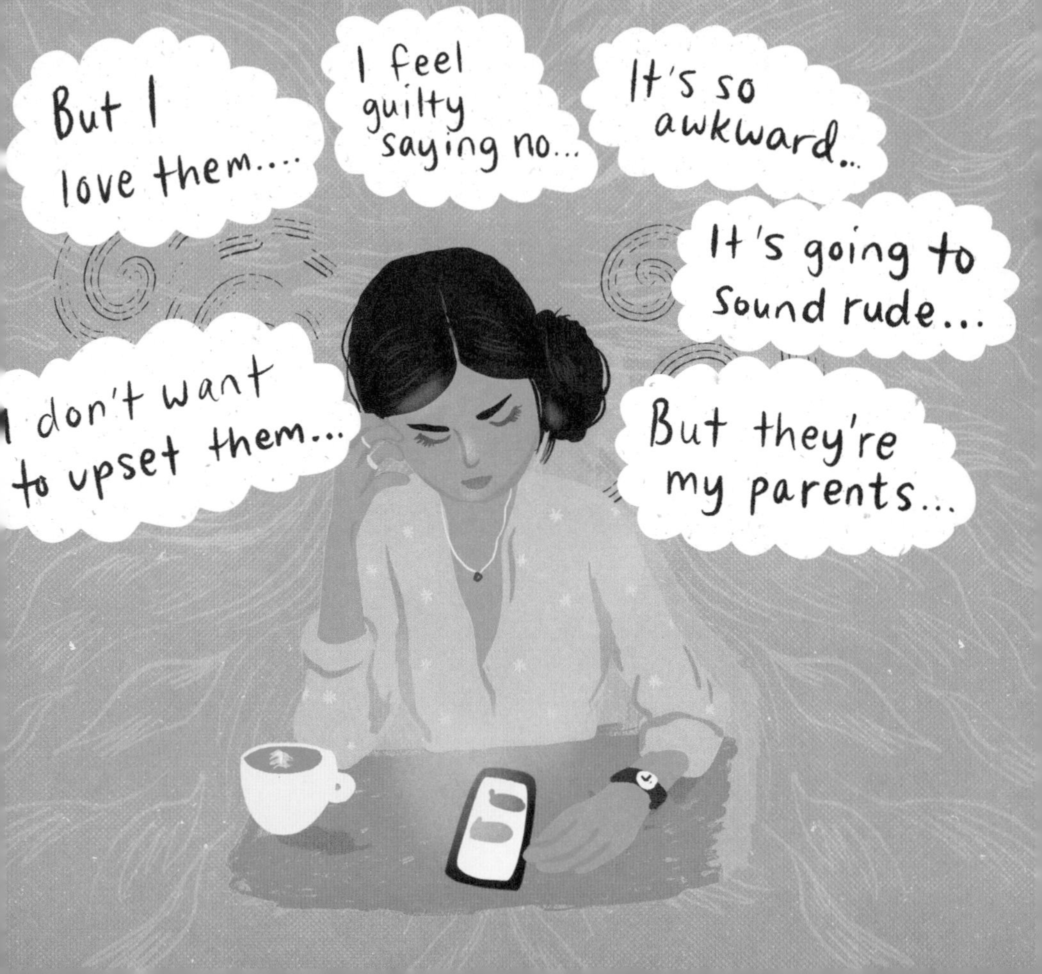

Loving your parents can look like:

Spending quality time with them

Setting healthy boundaries

Telling them how much you love them

Thanking them for their advice

We love our parents, but they def get on our nerves. You can love them (and let them know that!) while still forging your own path. List some ways you can be independent *and* stay connected.

Every family has its troubles, but some are just downright toxic. Describe a time when you put yourself first, and then write down why you know it was the right thing to do.

Dealing with toxic family situations

YOU ARE ALLOWED TO WALK AWAY

YOU ARE ALLOWED TO SET BOUNDARIES

YOU DON'T HAVE TO BE A SAVIOR DURING EVERY CRISIS

YOU DON'T NEED TO EXPLAIN YOUR SITUATION

YOU DON'T NEED THEIR APPROVAL TO BE SUCCESSFUL

What I love about my family

They inspire me

We cheer each other on

They're always there for me when I need them

They're honest with me

They teach me how to do things

They always know how to comfort me

They're not perfect, but they're yours! List some of the ways your unique family has made you *you*. What are you grateful for about your family?

WHAT I'M THINKING AND FEELING RIGHT NOW

Unrealistic expectations TV shows gave us about friendships

friendships are easy
and happen naturally

everyone has a close
group of friends who meet
up for coffee every day
and never drift apart

all friendships
last forever

friends will drop
anything, any time to
hang out with you

Let's Be Friends

Friendships are the glue that holds your life together! Tons of evidence shows that having strong friendships makes us happier and more resilient. But friendships do take some effort, so let's talk about how to be a good friend.

What's your friendship style? Are you the quiet but always supportive one? The party planner who remembers every birthday? The one they call for serious life advice? List some of the ways you practice being a good friend.

_____

_____

_____

_____

_____

_____

_____

_____

_____

_____

_____

_____

_____

_____

_____

_____

_____

_____

_____

_____

WHICH FRIEND ARE YOU?

#1 Sends the best memes

#2 sleeps in the latest

#3 most holiday spirit

#4 has the craziest stories

#5 weirdest Spotify playlists

#6 gives the best advice

A true friend is someone whose company makes you feel calm, confident, loved. Who are the friends you rely on? Describe how they make your life better.

Let's chat about your bestie. Having someone who really gets you is . . . everything. What do you love most about your BFF?

Why inside jokes are the best

They're like a secret language that most people can't understand

They bring back funny memories

Sometimes they don't even have to be funny

They can add a layer of intimacy to a relationship

They make us feel included

They help us form new friendships

One of the things that makes it clear your friendship was meant to be? Cracking up over something that no one else gets. Describe an inside joke you share with someone who means a lot to you.

Empathy is a superpower, but it can also make you extra vulnerable, so you have to use it wisely. Where do you fall on the empathy spectrum?

Signs you are an
EMPATH

YOU CAN FEEL OTHER PEOPLES' EMOTIONS

YOU HAVE TROUBLE SAYING NO

YOU HAVE ACCURATE INTUITION

YOU NEED TIME ALONE

YOU'RE A GOOD LISTENER

PEOPLE TELL YOU THEIR PROBLEMS

YOU ARE OVERWHELMED BY LARGE CROWDS

YOU ARE HIGHLY SENSITIVE

Why we go back to toxic friends

as time passes
we forget
how bad they
made us feel

we get
lonely

we think they
might have
changed

we are
people pleasers
and don't feel we
deserve something better

We become
comfortable and
used to their behavior

Sometimes we choose things—or people—that are not good for us because it feels familiar and we mistake that for feeling "right." Describe a toxic friendship you've experienced. Did you break free? If not, think about how you can protect yourself now.

Friendships can be fraught! And like all good things in life, they do take some work. If you have a fraying friendship, think about some ways you could mend it. Describe why you want to keep this friend in your life.

How to save a damaged friendship

REACH OUT, MAKE TIME TO TALK OPENLY AND HONESTLY.

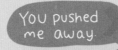

USE "I" STATEMENTS TO AVOID PUTTING THE BLAME ON THEM.

ASK THEM HOW THEY FEEL, AND <u>LISTEN</u>.

SPEND TIME TOGETHER AND TALK ABOUT HAPPY MEMORIES YOU SHARE.

DON'T FORCE IT — TIME IS THE BEST HEALER. YOU BOTH HAVE TO BE READY.

Signs you've outgrown a friend

both too
busy for plans

only talk
about past
memories
together

constant
arguing

awkward
conversations

opposing set
of values

feel drained
after spendin
time together

We all change and grow—and sometimes we grow apart. Being able to recognize when a friendship is over, and say goodbye with appreciation, shows respect for both of you and enables you to enjoy your memories of the relationship. Is there someone in your life you've outgrown? How could you gently tell them that you need to make some changes while acknowledging how much you have appreciated their friendship?

Being able to give a sincere compliment is a skill that will pay dividends throughout your life. Getting a compliment boosts the recipient's self-esteem and lets them know you care—plus it can also have a positive effect on your own mood. Practice below by writing detailed and genuine compliments to some friends. (Then actually tell them!)

How to give sincere compliments

Be specific—
it will be much
more memorable!
Character traits
and behaviors are
a good place to start.

Make sure they
are true and
heartfelt.

Avoid commenting
on someone's body.

Avoid using "I"
statements that
make it about
yourself.

Compliments are
so important—they
strengthen relationships,
break the ice, improve
self-esteem, and more.
Don't hold them back!

How to be a better friend

GIVE THEM
SPACE WHEN
THEY NEED IT

BUILD THEM UP

SET CLEAR
BOUNDARIES
WITH THEM

PRACTICE
JUST LISTENING
WITHOUT GIVIN
ADVICE

DON'T
LOSE
TOUCH WHEN
YOU ENTER
A NEW
RELATIONSHIP

APOLOGIZE
AND FORGIVE
AFTER ARGUMENTS

CHECK IN
CONSISTENTLY

Treasure your friendships and keep them healthy! Think about your most important relationships—are there any that could use a little bit of upkeep? Jot down your plans to do some friendship maintenance.

WHAT I'M THINKING AND FEELING RIGHT NOW

What's your dating personality?

THE GO-GETTER

- Is down for an adventure
- Thinks hike > coffee date
- Falls instantly in love

THE BLABBERING BABE

- Takes up 90% of the conversation
- Has a 2-hour date minimum
- Makes elite eye contac

THE QUEEN BEE

- Knows her worth
- Sets expectations within 10 seconds
- Takes her sweet time to reapply lipstick

THE DEEP DIVE DIVA

- Examines your birth chart
- Wants to know your therapist's #
- Will cry at least once

Navigating Love, Sex & Relationships

Having a healthy, rewarding romantic relationship takes work—but what's worth having that doesn't? Knowing and loving yourself makes it much likelier that you'll be able to create a loving relationship with someone else.

Yeah, I love a good rom-com, but they're not actually real. REAL relationships are messy, unexpected, and sometimes awkward and occasionally boring. That's the truth. What are some unrealistic expectations that you have harbored about relationships? What did the reality look like?

Unrealistic expectations rom-coms gave me

A close friend would profess their love for me

Frequent kisses in the rain

Ben & Jerry's would instantly cure heartbreak

Clean, perfect sex every time

Dramatic moments in airports

I'd fall in love with a billionaire, celebrity, vampire, etc.

Things you learn from dating the wrong person

YOUR WORTH!

HOW VALUABLE YOUR TIME REALLY IS

THE THINGS YOU NEED IN A PARTNER

NOT TO SETTLE!

THE THINGS YOU DON'T WANT IN A PARTNER

YOU CAN STILL HAVE FOND MEMORIES FROM A RELATIONSHIP THAT DOESN'T WORK OUT

HOW TO BE VULNERABLE

Not every relationship needs to last forever to be worthwhile. You probably have gone on some dates or tried out some relationships that taught you something valuable—what are some things you learned?

Everyone gets their heart broken at some point, and it can be extremely painful. Try to see it as a normal rite of passage instead of a failure. Whether you are the breaker or the breakee, it's not easy. List some ideas for healthy ways to move on.

How to get closure after a breakup

talk with friends

reflect without placing blame

focus on YOURSELF

change your environment

let yourself grieve

give it time

journal your feelings

How to get closure after being ghosted

END ALL CONTACT.

DON'T TAKE IT PERSONALLY! IT'S <u>NOT</u> SOMETHING YOU DID OR SAID.

TELL A FRIEND ABOUT WHAT HAPPENED. MANY PEOPLE EXPERIENCE THIS AND CAN HELP YOU THROUGH IT. YOU'RE NOT ALONE!

BE GENTLE ON YOURSELF GIVE YOURSELF TIME TO MOURN THE RELATIONSHIP YOU WANTED TO HAVE.

Being ghosted is and will always be gross. You feel invisible, unwanted, rejected. But it's really the ghoster's problem, isn't it? They're the coward who doesn't want to face you. Letting out your feelings will help! Describe how it feels to be ghosted. Then come up with three fun self-care activities to help yourself heal.

Being single is not a bad thing—you really are all you need! Jot down three cool things you have learned about yourself from being single and three fun things you like to do by yourself.

Unexpected benefits of being SINGLE

More time and energy to put into friendships

Stronger understanding of yourself and your interests

It's easier to stay focused on your personal goals

Can be more spontaneous

Spend less money!

It's a great feeling to know that all you need to feel whole and happy is you!

When you're having a good time with someone, notice what it feels like. Mindfulness + dating = fulfilling relationships. Write down how it feels when you're really enjoying someone's company.

No one is perfect, but being with someone who is (mostly) emotionally healthy feels waaay better than toughing it out with someone who needs to work on themselves. Who are you when you're with someone who's good for your mental health? How are you good for them?

Signs someone is good for your mental health

There's no competition between the 2 of you

They listen to you with empathy

They always respect your boundaries

You feel like the best version of yourself around them

They ask you questions and want to know more about you

They are open and honest with you and don't judge

How a good partner makes you feel

HAPPY

UNDERSTOOD

RESPECTED

SEXY

INTERESTING

SAFE

LOVED

COMFORTABLE

SUPPORTED

STRONG

FUNNY

EXCITED

SPECIAL

The best part of any relationship is getting to spend time with someone who knows you intimately—every secret and quirk. Describe how it feels when you're with someone who really gets you.

WHAT I'M THINKING AND FEELING RIGHT NOW

What do you daydream about?

MY CRUSH

PIZZA

CONVERSATIONS I WANT TO HAPPEN

NEW JOB

SIPPING TEA AND READING A GOOD BOOK

BEING FAMOUS

WATCHING NETFLIX IN BED WITH A FLUFFY BLANKET AND MY DOG

TRYING OUT NEW SKINCARE PRODUCTS

VACATIONS

DONUTS

HAVING SUPERPOWERS

Fulfilling My Dreams

Daydreaming is way underappreciated. Imagining yourself in the near or far future doing something you love is a great way to be kind to and motivate yourself. What might your future hold?

What would you do if you weren't scared and you knew it would work out? Make a list—don't hold back!

TIPS for actually pursuing your dreams
PUT YOURSELF OUT THERE
REALLY BELIEVE THEY WILL HAPPEN
IGNORE THE SKEPTICS
WRITE OUT SPECIFIC GOALS
START, LEARN FROM YOUR MISTAKES, AND KEEP GOING!
SURROUND YOURSELF WITH PEOPLE WHO BELIEVE IN YOU

How to stop saying "sorry"
Some better alternatives

When you make a mistake, say "How can I fix this?"

Instead of "I'm sorry, I forgot" say "thank you for reminding me."

Instead of "Sorry to bother you" say "thanks for taking the time to help me with this."

Use "Unfortunately." Ex.: "Unfortunately, I'm not available" instead of "Sorry, I can't."

Apologizing when it's called for is a necessary skill. Over-apologizing, however, is not good for you. It makes real apologies seem less sincere and undermines your confidence. Jot down some times when you tend to apologize unnecessarily. What could you say instead?

Creativity is bravery! Instead of worrying about how your efforts will be received, go ahead and dream, imagine, and express yourself. Use this page to jot down some ideas you'd like to explore.

How to feed your CREATIVITY

happiness and motivation bring out the highest levels of creativity (NOT sadness)

get in the habit of writing down ideas as they come to you, without judgment

spend time with creative people

be willing to explore and try new things

daydream often

spend time in nature

get enough sleep!

take a shower or go for a walk! let your mind wander — it's good for creativity

exercise

What does passion look like?

- losing track of time
- obsessing over improving
- a reason to wake up in the morning
- a lot of hard work
- trying again after each setback
- believing in yourself no matter what

Your best work often comes from being in what psychologists call a state of "flow," when you're utterly absorbed in what you're doing and it feels great. That's passion. What activities make you feel this way?

I procrastinate all the time, usually when there is something I'm unsure about how to do or when I'm worried about how it will turn out. Breaking a task into smaller steps usually helps me get started. Think of a recent time you put off doing something—can you figure out why you felt that way? How could you break it down into more manageable parts?

How to avoid
PROCRASTINATION

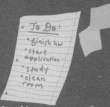

Make a
To-Do List

Set a
Schedule

Tell others
about your goals

Visualize
yourself working
and finishing your
tasks

Reward
yourself

How to MIX UP your routine

Wear an outfit you don't wear often

Try a new recipe you find online

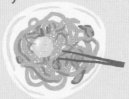

Redecorate your workspace

Try watching a movie or a TV show in a different language

Style your hair differently

Watch the sunset or sunrise

A refresh or a change in your routine is a great way to give yourself a creativity and/or mood boost! What are some ideas you have for shaking up your regular regimen?

Intentions are powerful! Planning your path and envisioning what you want can help you achieve it. Write down in detail how you'd like to see an upcoming project or event play out.

What manifesting can look like

Closing your eyes and pretending you already have the thing you are manifesting

keeping a gratitude Journal to record things bring you closer to your goals

Using present-tense affirmations ("I have", not "I want")

making Vision boards

How to actually stop comparing yourself to others

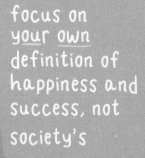

don't fall for the illusion of scarcity— when others do well it does <u>not</u> mean there is less for you

focus on <u>your own</u> definition of happiness and success, not society's

realize you are comparing your <u>real life</u> & <u>imperfections</u> to their <u>highlight reel</u>

remember that no one person is better than another

Yes, comparison really is the thief of joy. Focus on what you have to offer and don't worry about what other people are doing. List five to ten things you do well and why you enjoy doing them. How can you share them with others?

Rather than focusing on ticking off the boxes, think of accomplishment as a state of being, when you are doing things you truly enjoy and finding meaning and pleasure in doing them. What are those things for you?

What does Accomplishment feel like?

pride

happiness

a confidence boost

maybe I could have done better

gratitude

NOW WHAT ? – feelings of anxiety and emptiness

reflecting on your journey

WHAT I'M THINKING AND FEELING RIGHT NOW

CONFIDENCE 2.0

no longer interested in comparing yourself to others

positive affirmations

an outfit you feel yourself in

not afraid to say "no" to things that no longer serve you

fake it 'til you make it!

letting go of the need to be perfect

unafraid to stand out and let your true personality shine through